God Created You Exactly Right

Christine Harder Tangvald
Illustrated by Steve Henry

Chariot Books™ is an imprint of David C. Cook Publishing Co.
David C. Cook Publishing Co., Elgin, Illinois 60120
David C. Cook Publishing Co., Weston, Ontario
Nova Distribution Ltd., Torquay, England

GOD CREATED YOU EXACTLY RIGHT

©1991 by Christine Harder Tangvald for text and Steve Henry for illustrations.
All rights reserved.
Cover and interior design by Therese Cooper
First Printing, 1991. Printed in the United States of America
95 94 93 92 91 5 4 3 2 1
ISBN 1-55513-489-0 LC 91-70858

Chariot Books™
David C. Cook Publishing Co.

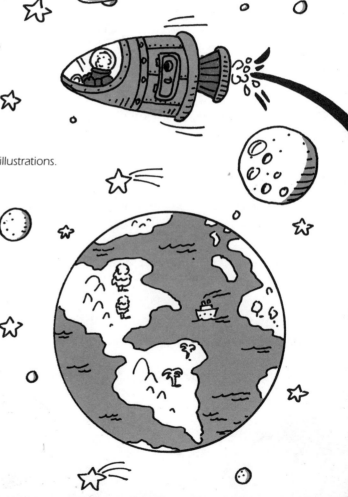

Let's Have Some Fun!

HELLO THERE!

My name is **Christine**.
What is **your** name?

Well, HOW DO YOU DO, _____! I'm really glad to meet you.

Would you like to have some FUN with me, and go through this book together? You would! Oh, good. I'd like that. I'd like that a LOT!

You know, _____,
there's something I've been wondering about for a long, long time.
And MAYBE you have been wondering about it, too.

I wonder—do you think it was hard for God to make our WHOLE, WIDE WORLD?

And **how** did our wonderful world **get here**, anyway?
That's what I want to know!

How did God know EXACTLY what to do?

I mean, what if God had made a whole bunch of MISTAKES??!!

Like, what if God FORGOT to create the SUN!
It would be dark all the time, and we would **freeze** to death. . . .
BRRRRRRR!

And what if He made all the water HOT—BOILING HOT?!
What then? All the fish would die, and we couldn't take a bath
or even get a DRINK! Too HOT!

And what if God accidentally put a HUGE hippopotamus's head
on top of a tiny ant's body?

Oh, NO! It would squish itself to death! Wouldn't that be AWFUL?

But God DID NOT make any mistakes! Oh, no, He did not! He DID NOT forget to create the sun.
He did not make all the water boiling hot or put a hippopotamus's head on top of an ant's body.
Oh, no. Because GOD IS GOD and God DOES NOT make mistakes. No, He does not!
God created EVERYTHING in our whole wide world . . . **exactly right**!

Let's start at the very beginning, OK?
Close your eyes. What do you see?
Nothing. Absolutely nothing.

NOTHING

ABSOLUTLY NOTHING

That's what there was before God made the world.
Nothing at ALL!

And then, the Bible tells us:

VERSE
TIME

"In the beginning God created
the heaven and the earth."
(Genesis 1:1)

And God made them . . . EXACTLY RIGHT!

Dear God,
I'm glad **You** are GOD.
I'm glad You do not make mistakes. You can't make mistakes, can You—because **You** are GOD!
Thank You for making the heaven and the earth.
Thank You for making everything . . . EXACTLY RIGHT!
Amen

GOOD-BYE TIME

I'm so glad you are going through this book with me. You and I are going to have **lots** of fun finding out about all the AMAZING things God created.
And each one is . . . **exactly right**!
See you **next time**. Good-bye!

SOMETHING FUN-TO-DO

1. Carefully cut out the BEAUTIFUL BIBLE BOOKMARK in the back of this book. Have someone help you find Genesis 1:1 in your Bible, and put your bookmark right into your very own Bible.

2. Cut out the **heaven** picture piece from page 23, and glue it on OUR WONDERFUL WORLD picture on the inside cover. Each time we will add something to OUR WONDERFUL WORLD picture until it is . . . **exactly right**!

A Trip through Space

HELLO TIME

HELLO, AGAIN!

I'm so glad you came back to have some more FUN with me!
Would you like to go on a SPACE TRIP today? You would?
GOOD! Let's get started!

Do you remember what our Bible memory verse says?

VERSE TIME

"In the beginning God created
the heaven and the earth."
(Genesis 1:1)

Wow! When God created the HEAVEN, that was ONE BIG JOB!
You see, God created **hundreds** of stars— **thousands** of stars—
millions and **billions** and **trillions** of stars!

He put some over here. He put some over there.
He put planets and moons and stars EVERYWHERE!
And then KERPLUNK! God put the earth RIGHT HERE . . .
exactly where He wanted it to be! Isn't that amazing?

And KERPLUNK! God put the SUN way out there . . .
exactly where He wanted it to be.

God's sun shines and shines and shines.
Do you know why it shines and shines and shines?
Because God's sun is HOT!
It is hot, **hot**, HOT, HOT!

The sun is SO HOT, it is hotter than a FIRE! Did you know that?

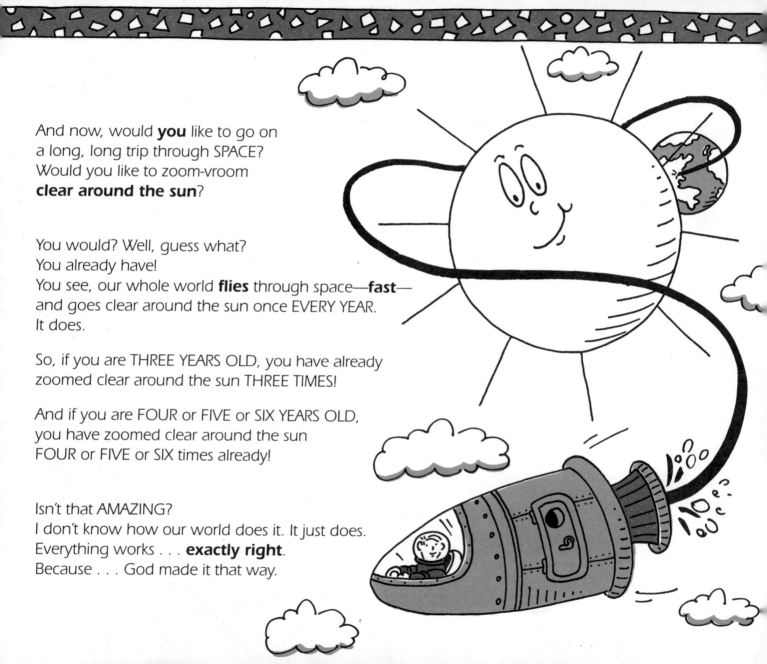

And now, would **you** like to go on
a long, long trip through SPACE?
Would you like to zoom-vroom
clear around the sun?

You would? Well, guess what?
You already have!
You see, our whole world **flies** through space—**fast**—
and goes clear around the sun once EVERY YEAR.
It does.

So, if you are THREE YEARS OLD, you have already
zoomed clear around the sun THREE TIMES!

And if you are FOUR or FIVE or SIX YEARS OLD,
you have zoomed clear around the sun
FOUR or FIVE or SIX times already!

Isn't that AMAZING?
I don't know how our world does it. It just does.
Everything works . . . **exactly right**.
Because . . . God made it that way.

PRAYER TIME

Dear God,
You are AMAZING.
How did You make the sun and earth
and all the stars?
HOW DID YOU DO IT?
God, I **like** your heaven and earth.
Thank You for creating them . . . exactly right!
Amen

GOOD-BYE TIME

Hasn't this been FUN—spinning and zooming
through space together? WOW! I can hardly wait
to see what else God created! I'll be waiting for you.
Good-bye!

SOMETHING FUN-TO-DO

1. Cut out the **sun** on page 23 and glue it onto the sky in
   OUR WONDERFUL WORLD picture.

2. Pretend you are **zooming** around the sun in your own spaceship.
   You can use a cardboard box or a chair or your trike or bike.
   Don't get lost out there in space! ZOOM . . . VROOM!

Busy, Busy, BUSY!

Hi!
I'm **so glad** to see you again. Did you have fun pretending to ZOOM through space? I did.

If you think God was busy when He created the HEAVEN, just wait until you see what He did when He created the EARTH!

Do you remember our Bible memory verse?

"In the beginning
God created the heaven
and the earth."
(Genesis 1:1)

Well, God got busy, BUSY, **BUSY**!

God created WATER—lots and lots of water.

He made rivers and streams and huge oceans

with waves that slap the shore:

Ker-SPLASH, Ker-SPLASH, Ker-SPLASH!

God put fish and sea creatures into His magnificent ocean.
Big fish and little fish.
Fast fish and slow fish
FUNNY FISH and SCARY FISH!
Swish! Swish! go God's fish!

And high in His blue, blue sky,
God made INCREDIBLE BIRDS . . .
that FLY!

He made birds that cheep and peep—like robins!

He made birds that gawk and squawk—like sea gulls!

He made birds that swoop and loop—like buzzards!

He made beautiful birds and funny birds and birds
that sing and sing and sing—like CANARIES!

Oh, yes, God was very busy. BUSY, BUSY, BUSY!

And in God's new land,
He planted seeds.

He made carrot seeds and radish seeds.

He made seeds for pumpkins and corn and beans.

He planted apples and oranges.

He planted roses and lilacs and daisies . . . and even the CACTUS!

God planted short green grass and tall green trees.

God created all the plants on earth.

And when He finished,
He looked over the sky and ocean and the land.
And God said, "THIS IS GOOD."
And IT WAS!

PRAYER TIME

Dear God,
Thank You for making our wonderful world so special.
My favorite thing about Your wonderful world is _____ .
Thank You, God, for making everything . . . **exactly right**!
Amen

Would you like to know some more AMAZING things about God's wonderful earth? You would? Oh, good. Then I will see you NEXT TIME. Good-bye!

GOOD-BYE TIME

SOMETHING FUN-TO-DO

1. Glue the **fish**, **birds**, **trees**, and **flowers** on page 23 onto OUR WONDERFUL WORLD picture.

2. Create your own FISH! Draw a picture of it. Give your fish a name.

3. Cut one to two inches off the top of a carrot with green leaves. Place the top in a shallow dish with one inch of water. Set your carrot top on a windowsill and watch the green leaves grow, grow, GROW!

God's Amazing Animals

Oh, hi there. I've been waiting for you. Do you know why?
Because today is an EXCITING day to learn what God did next!

Remember, our Bible verse says,

HELLO TIME

VERSE TIME

"In the beginning God created the heaven and the earth."
(Genesis 1:1)

But, you see, God wasn't **done** with our wonderful world. Not yet. He knew
our world needed some **animals**—lots and lots of AMAZING ANIMALS!

See if you can name some of these amazing animals that God created.

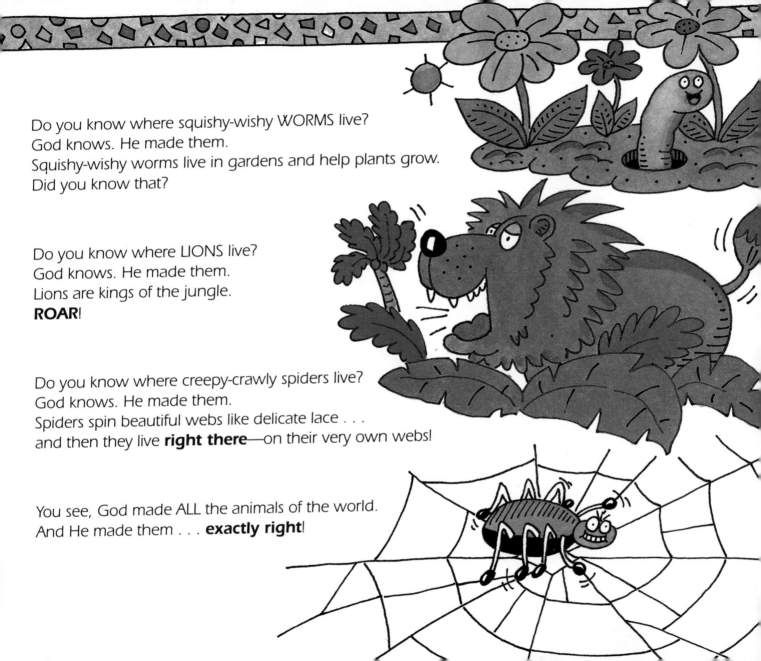

Do you know where squishy-wishy WORMS live?
God knows. He made them.
Squishy-wishy worms live in gardens and help plants grow.
Did you know that?

Do you know where LIONS live?
God knows. He made them.
Lions are kings of the jungle.
ROAR!

Do you know where creepy-crawly spiders live?
God knows. He made them.
Spiders spin beautiful webs like delicate lace . . .
and then they live **right there**—on their very own webs!

You see, God made ALL the animals of the world.
And He made them . . . **exactly right**!

He made SNAKES that go slither, slither, slither.
Did you know that snakes can crawl **right out** of their very own skins?!
They can.
God made them that way.

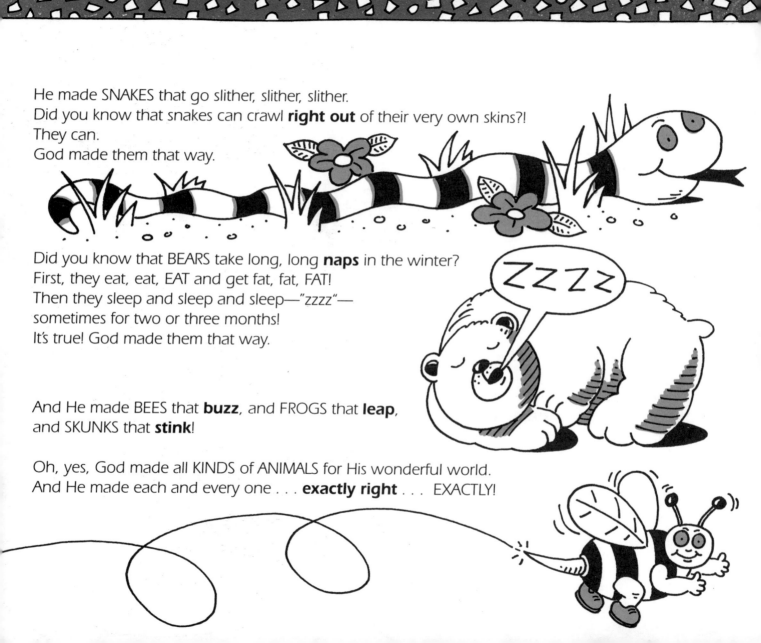

Did you know that BEARS take long, long **naps** in the winter?
First, they eat, eat, EAT and get fat, fat, FAT!
Then they sleep and sleep and sleep—"zzzz"—
sometimes for two or three months!
It's true! God made them that way.

And He made BEES that **buzz**, and FROGS that **leap**,
and SKUNKS that **stink**!

Oh, yes, God made all KINDS of ANIMALS for His wonderful world.
And He made each and every one . . . **exactly right** . . . EXACTLY!

PRAYER TIME

Dear God,
How did You do it?
How did You **think up** all Your
wonderful animals?
I think You are **smart**, God.
Amen

GOOD-BYE TIME

God looked at all His animals and said,
"THIS IS GOOD!" And it was.
But God wasn't done yet!
Next time, we will see God's BEST creation of all.
Because, God saved the BEST for LAST!

See you then. Good-bye!

SOMETHING FUN-TO-DO

1. Glue the **animals** from page 23 onto
   OUR WONDERFUL WORLD picture.

2. Create your own animal. Draw a picture of
   your animal. Give your animal a neat name!

3. Pretend to be a frog, a fish, an elephant, a snake,
   a rabbit or a _____. HAVE FUN!

The Best for Last

HELLO TIME

Hello, again! Boy, am I **excited** about today. I hope YOU are, too.

I have another question. I wonder if you know the answer.
Why do you think God went to SO MUCH WORK to create our
whole wide world? Why did He want to make EVERYTHING . . . **exactly right**?

Well, God had a very good reason.
You see, He wasn't done yet!
God saved His most AMAZING creation of all for LAST!

VERSE TIME

"In the beginning God created
the heaven and earth."
(Genesis 1:1)

Well, God looked all over His heaven and His earth.
But, something was **missing**.
Something **important**.
"I know what is missing!" said God.
Then, carefully, carefully, God scooped up some clay—
and gently, gently . . . HE MADE . . .

A MAN!

He DID! GOD MADE A MAN!
How could He DO that?
He could do it because He is GOD!

God made the man a **lot** like Himself—in His own divine image.

And THEN do you know what God did?
He BREATHED right into the man—"Whhh, Whhh"—
the breath of LIFE! And man became a living soul!

WOW!

I wish I could have seen God do that!

But God wasn't done yet. No, He wasn't!
He didn't want His MAN to be all alone,
so, God created . . . (can you guess?) . . .

A WOMAN!

WOW!
God created a woman!

And God loved His MAN and His WOMAN.
He loved them a lot!
He loved them **so much** that He put them in charge
of all the rest of the WHOLE WIDE WORLD.

"You shall have dominion!" God said.
"Please take good care of My world."

So you see, THAT'S why God **worked** and **worked** to
make our wonderful world . . . EXACTLY RIGHT!
He wanted everything to be perfect for His MAN
and His WOMAN!
AND IT WAS.

And GUESS WHAT!

God made YOU and ME **exactly right**, too.

He loves us. He does.
And He wants everything to be **exactly right** for US.

He wants us to take good care of His wonderful world—
His amazing animals
His blue, blue sky
God's oceans and rivers and streams
His tall, tall mountains
All the birds and the fish He made.

We NEED to take GOOD care of ALL of God's
wonderful world, don't we?
Because God created it . . .
EXACTLY RIGHT . . . for **you** and for **me**!

PRAYER TIME

Dear God,
Thank You for our wonderful world.
You made EVERYTHING exactly right—
EXACTLY RIGHT—for ME.
Thank You, God. Thank You for everything.
Amen

SOMETHING FUN-TO-DO

1. Glue the **man** and **woman** from page 23 onto the OUR WONDERFUL WORLD picture. Hang your nice picture where you will see it often.

2. Draw your own picture of God's wonderful world. Draw a picture of your wonderful self in God's wonderful world. (I wish I could see your picture.)

GOOD-BYE TIME

I think YOU are SO SPECIAL! God made you that way, **exactly right**, you know. Thank you so much for reading this book with me.

I had **fun**. I hope you did, too. Maybe we can read **another** Fun-to-Do Devotion book together sometime! I'd like that. I'd like it a lot. Would you? Oh, GOOD! I'll see you then. Take care, and GOOD-BYE, **special friend**.

With much love from

Dear Parents,

I'm so glad you have chosen this Fun-to-Do Devotions book to do with your child and with **me**! You won't need much time to go through these fun devotions, but be sure the time is as regular as possible—maybe after a meal or after nap time.

You don't need many things to start out, just this book and the Bible and whatever the devotion suggests to make it a really fun time for you and your child.

Each devotion uses the same elements. In each one you'll find:
- ■ HELLO TIME
- ■ PRAYER TIME
- ■ VERSE TIME
- ■ GOOD-BYE TIME
- ■ SOMETHING FUN TO DO

Because young children learn well through repetition, the same Scripture verse is used in each devotion. By the time you finish this book, your child will probably have memorized the verse.

When you finish this book, look for more Fun-to-Do Devotions at your local Christian bookstore.

I promise—these devotions will be fun for both you and your child!

God Bless!

Christine